CHICKEN

WILTON HOUSE

Editor Angela Rahaniotis
Graphic Design Zapp
Photography Marc Bruneau
Food Preparation /Stylist Josée Robitaille
Assistant Stylist Marc Maula

Wilton House is an imprint
of Joshua Morris Publishing Inc.,
221 Danbury Road, Wilton, CT 06897

10 9 8 7 6 5 4 3 2 1
ISBN: 0-88705-839-6

CHICKEN

Chicken is an all-time family favorite.
And because it is inexpensive, and
low in fat and calories, it is the perfect
choice for the budget-minded and
health-conscious cook.

But as the great chefs know, chicken
is also one of the most versatile of meats.
This book contains a tantalizing
selection of chicken dishes, ranging
from the quick and simple to
the exotic and elegant.

As an added bonus, you'll find easy,
step-by-step methods for cutting up
whole chickens and boning chicken
breasts – money-saving techniques that
every good cook should master.

With food this good at your fingertips,
your family may insist on chicken
several times a week!

How to Cut Up Chicken

1 Pulling the leg gently away from the chicken with one hand, cut through the skin connecting the leg to the body. Twist the leg away from its natural position until the joint cracks. Cut through the joint with a sharp knife.

2 Place the leg, skin side down, and cut through the joint to separate the drumstick from the thigh. Repeat with second leg.

3 Hold the wing away from the body and pull firmly until the joint cracks. Cut through the joint to separate the wing from the body.

4 Insert the knife blade between the rib cage and backbone to cut the breast from the carcass.

5 Cut the chicken breast in half lengthwise to make two chicken supremes.

6 You will have six chicken pieces. Cut each breast in half if you want to make eight portions.

Boning Chicken Supremes

1 Pull the skin off the chicken pieces.

2 Insert the knife blade between the chicken flesh and the piece of cartilage which runs the length of each breast half. Cut along the cartilage, pulling the flesh gently away with the other hand.

Tips for Preparing Chicken

- All chicken should be rinsed under cold water and dried thoroughly with paper towels before proceeding. Work on a surface that can be washed and sterilized.

- A chicken cut in 6 pieces yields:
  2 breast halves
  2 drumsticks
  2 thighs

- A chicken cut in 8 pieces yields:
  4 breast pieces
  2 drumsticks
  2 thighs

- The size of chicken pieces can vary. Use the cooking times as a guideline only, and adjust time according to size.

Chicken Stock

1 lb	chicken bones	500 g
6 cups	water	1.5 L
½ cup	chopped carrot	125 mL
½ cup	chopped onion	125 mL
½ cup	chopped celery	125 mL
½ cup	chopped leek	125 mL
1	garlic clove, crushed	1
1	sprig thyme	1
1	bay leaf	1
10	whole peppercorns	10
1	clove	1

1 Rinse the chicken bones and put them in a stock pot. Add the water and bring to a boil. Using a spoon, skim off the foam that forms on the surface.

2 Add the remaining ingredients and let simmer over low heat for 1½ hours. The liquid should bubble very gently.

3 Skim off the fat and strain the stock. Let cool and store refrigerated.

Spanish Chicken
(4 servings)

3½ lb	cleaned chicken, cut in 6 pieces	1.6 kg
2 tbsp	olive oil	30 mL
1	onion, peeled and chopped	1
2	garlic cloves, peeled, crushed and chopped	2
¼ lb	frozen green peas	125 g
2	slices back bacon, cooked and cut in julienne	2
2	yellow bell peppers	2
2	red bell peppers	2
2	tomatoes, cored and halved	2
1 tbsp	chopped fresh parsley	15 mL
	salt and pepper	

1 Skin chicken pieces and season well. Heat 2 tbsp (30 mL) oil in sauté pan over medium heat. Add chicken. Cook 18 minutes over low heat, turning pieces over 2 to 3 times.

2 Remove chicken breasts from pan and set aside.

3 Add onion and garlic to pan with remaining chicken; continue cooking 8 minutes. Return chicken breasts to pan and add peas and bacon. Cook 4 minutes.

4 Meanwhile, cut bell peppers in half and remove seeds. Oil skin and place cut-side-down on cookie sheet. Oil cut sides of tomatoes and place cut-side-up on cookie sheet. Broil 8 to 10 minutes. Peel off skin from peppers.

5 Serve chicken with roasted bell peppers and tomatoes. Sprinkle with parsley. Accompany with rice, if desired.

Rolled Chicken Breasts with Prosciutto and Cheese
(4 servings)

2	whole boneless chicken breasts	2
4	slices prosciutto	4
4	slices Gruyère cheese	4
3 tbsp	butter	45 mL
2	carrots, pared and sliced	2
2	shallots, peeled and thinly sliced	2
1½ cups	chicken stock, heated	375 mL
1 tbsp	cornstarch	15 mL
3 tbsp	cold water	45 mL
	salt and pepper	

Preheat oven to 350°F (180°C).

1 Skin chicken, split into halves and remove fat. Using wooden mallet or rolling pin, flatten breasts between two sheets of waxed paper. Breasts should be about ¼ in (5 mm) thick.

2 Season chicken and place flat on work surface. Cover each with slice of prosciutto and slice of cheese. Tuck edges of meat over filling, then roll and secure with string.

3 Heat butter in ovenproof sauté pan over medium heat. Add chicken rolls, carrots and shallots; season well. Sear 3 minutes, browning rolls on all sides.

4 Cover and finish cooking in oven for 8 to 10 minutes or adjust time according to size.

5 When chicken is cooked, remove rolls from pan and set aside on heated serving platter.

6 Place pan on stove over high heat. Pour in chicken stock and cook 3 minutes.

7 Dilute cornstarch in cold water. Stir into sauce and cook 1 minute over low heat. Serve sauce over chicken. Accompany with potatoes and zucchini, if desired.

Using wooden mallet or rolling pin, flatten breasts between two sheets of waxed paper. Breasts should be about ¼ in (5 mm) thick.

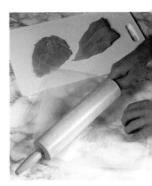

Cover each with slice of prosciutto and slice of cheese.

Tuck edges of meat over filling, then roll and secure with string.

Heat butter in ovenproof sauté pan over medium heat. Add chicken rolls, carrots and shallots; season well. Sear 3 minutes, browning rolls on all sides.

Stuffed Chicken Breasts Supreme
(4 servings)

2	whole boneless chicken breasts	2
1 cup	pitted Kalamata olives	250 mL
4	anchovy fillets, rinsed and drained	4
1 tbsp	lime juice	15 mL
1	garlic clove, peeled, crushed and chopped	1
1 tbsp	olive oil	15 mL
1 tbsp	Dijon mustard	15 mL
2	hard-boiled eggs, halved	2
3 tbsp	butter	45 mL
1 cup	dry white wine	250 mL
1 tbsp	chopped fresh basil	15 mL
	salt and pepper	

Preheat oven to 350°F (180°C).

1 Skin chicken, split into halves and remove fat. Using wooden mallet, flatten breasts between two sheets of waxed paper. Breasts should be about ¼ in (5 mm) thick. Season chicken and refrigerate.

2 Place olives, anchovies, lime juice, garlic, oil and mustard in food processor. Force eggs through wire sieve; add to food processor. Blend 30 seconds to purée.

3 Place chicken breasts flat on work surface. Spread equal amount of stuffing over each chicken breast. Roll and secure with string.

4 Heat butter in ovenproof sauté pan over medium heat. Add chicken rolls and sear 3 minutes, browning on all sides.

5 Cover and finish cooking in oven for 8 to 10 minutes or adjust time according to size.

6 When chicken is cooked, remove rolls from pan and set aside on heated serving platter.

7 Place pan on stove over high heat. Add wine and basil; cook 3 minutes.

8 Serve deglazed juices with chicken. Accompany with pasta, if desired.

Honey-Sweet Marinated Chicken Breasts
(4 servings)

2	whole boneless chicken breasts	2
3 tbsp	herb wine vinegar	45 mL
1½ tbsp	honey	25 mL
2 tbsp	Worcestershire sauce	30 mL
2 tsp	olive oil	10 mL
1	garlic clove, peeled, crushed and chopped	1
¼ tsp	oregano	1 mL
	pinch of thyme	
	freshly ground pepper	

1 Skin chicken and split into halves. Place in baking dish with all remaining ingredients. Cover with plastic wrap and refrigerate 1 hour.

2 Preheat oven to 400°F (200°C).

3 Transfer chicken breasts to ovenproof baking dish. Change oven setting to broil. When upper element is hot, place chicken in oven on top rack. Broil 5 minutes.

4 Reduce oven setting to 350°F (180°C). Turn chicken breasts over and bake 10 to 12 minutes or adjust time according to size. Turn breasts over again halfway through cooking.

5 Serve with garden salad or on toasted buns as hearty sandwiches.

Tarragon Baked Chicken Breasts
(4 servings)

2	**whole boneless chicken breasts**	2
2 tbsp	**butter**	30 mL
4	**sprigs fresh tarragon**	4
1 1/2 cups	**chicken stock, heated**	375 mL
1 tbsp	**cornstarch**	15 mL
3 tbsp	**cold water**	45 mL
1 cup	**frozen green peas**	250 mL
	juice of 1/2 lemon	
	salt and pepper	

Preheat oven to 350°F (180°C).

1 Skin chicken and split into halves. Heat butter in frying pan over medium heat. Add chicken breasts and cook 2 minutes on each side.

2 Place chicken breasts in single layer in ovenproof baking dish. Season well and add tarragon and lemon juice. Cover with foil and cook 18 minutes in oven.

3 Remove chicken from baking dish and set aside.

4 Place baking dish on stove over high heat. Pour in chicken stock and cook 3 minutes.

5 Dilute cornstarch in cold water; stir into sauce. Reduce heat to medium and cook 30 seconds.

6 Add peas and chicken breasts. Simmer 3 minutes over low heat, then serve. Accompany with asparagus and puréed sweet potatoes, if desired.

Chicken and Mushroom Caps
(4 servings)

3½ lb	cleaned chicken, cut in 8 pieces	1.6 kg
3 tbsp	olive oil	45 mL
12	shallots, peeled	12
½ lb	fresh mushroom caps, cleaned and quartered	225 g
3 tbsp	balsamic vinegar	45 mL
1½ cups	chicken stock, heated	375 mL
1 tbsp	cornstarch	15 mL
3 tbsp	cold water	45 mL
1 tbsp	chopped fresh parsley	15 mL
	salt and pepper	

1 Skin chicken pieces and season well. Heat oil in sauté pan over medium heat. Add chicken and shallots. Cook 18 minutes over low heat, turning pieces over 2 to 3 times.

2 Remove chicken breasts from pan and set aside.

3 Continue cooking remaining chicken in pan 5 minutes. Add mushroom caps, season and cook 8 minutes or until chicken is cooked. Remove chicken pieces and set aside.

4 Sprinkle in vinegar and increase heat to high; cook 2 minutes. Pour in chicken stock and continue cooking 2 minutes.

5 Dilute cornstarch in cold water; stir into pan. Return all chicken to pan and simmer 3 to 4 minutes over low heat.

6 Sprinkle with parsley and serve. Accompany with asparagus and polenta, if desired.

Chicken with Italian Sausage and Wine
(4 servings)

3½ lb	cleaned chicken, cut in 6 pieces	1.6 kg
2 tbsp	olive oil	30 mL
1	green bell pepper	1
1	yellow bell pepper	1
2	Italian sausages	2
2	garlic cloves, peeled, crushed and chopped	2
1	small onion, peeled and sliced in rings	1
½ cup	Chianti wine	125 mL
	salt and pepper	

1 Skin chicken pieces and season well. Heat 2 tbsp (30 mL) of oil in sauté pan over medium heat. Add chicken. Cook 18 minutes over low heat, turning pieces over 2 to 3 times.

2 Meanwhile, cut bell peppers in half and remove seeds. Oil skin and place cut-side-down on cookie sheet; broil 8 to 10 minutes in oven. Remove from oven and let cool. Peel off skin, slice peppers and set aside.

3 Slice sausages on the bias no thicker than ½ in (1 cm).

4 Remove chicken breasts from pan and set aside.

5 Add sliced bell peppers, sausages, garlic and onion to pan with remaining chicken. Season and cook 8 minutes over low heat.

6 Return chicken breasts to pan and continue cooking 4 minutes. Transfer chicken pieces to heated serving platter.

7 Add wine to mixture in pan. Cook 3 minutes over high heat. Pour over chicken and serve.

Sake-Marinated Fried Chicken
(4 to 6 servings)

2	whole boneless chicken breasts	2
2 tbsp	chopped fresh ginger	30 mL
¼ cup	soy sauce	50 mL
¼ cup	sake wine	50 mL
1 cup	cornstarch	250 mL
	few drops of hot pepper sauce	
	freshly ground pepper	
	vegetable oil for frying	

1 Skin chicken and cut into pieces 1 in (2.5 cm) wide.

2 Place in bowl with ginger, soy sauce, sake, hot pepper sauce and freshly ground pepper. Toss, cover and marinate 30 minutes.

3 Drain chicken pieces and dredge in cornstarch.

4 Heat vegetable oil in deep sauté pan over high heat. When hot, add chicken and fry over high heat until browned and cooked through.

5 Season with pepper and serve. Accompany with green beans, cucumbers and puréed sweet potatoes, if desired.

Curried Chicken Meatballs

(4 servings)

1 ½ lb	ground chicken	700 g
2 tbsp	breadcrumbs	30 mL
1 tbsp	chopped fresh parsley	15 mL
1	small egg	1
¼ cup	olive oil	50 mL
2	onions, peeled and thinly sliced	2
2 tbsp	curry powder	30 mL
1 tsp	cumin	5 mL
2 tbsp	flour	30 mL
2 cups	chicken stock, heated	500 mL
	few drops of Worcestershire sauce	
	few drops of Tabasco sauce	
	salt and pepper	

1 Place ground chicken, bread-crumbs, Worcestershire and Tabasco sauces and parsley in food processor. Blend briefly. Add egg and season with salt and pepper. Blend again until mixture takes shape and starts to form ball.

2 Shape mixture by hand into small meatballs, cover and refrigerate 15 minutes or until firm.

3 Heat half of oil in sauté pan over medium heat. Add meatballs and cook 4 to 5 minutes, browning on all sides. When cooked, remove meatballs and set aside to drain on paper towel.

4 Add remaining oil to pan. When hot, cook onions 12 minutes over low heat. Stir in curry powder and cumin; continue cooking 5 minutes.

5 Sprinkle in flour and mix well. Stir in chicken stock and cook 4 minutes over medium-low heat.

6 Return meatballs to pan, mix and simmer 4 minutes. Serve.

Chicken Legs with Fresh Fennel Bulb
(4 servings)

1	large fennel bulb	1
4	chicken legs	4
2 tbsp	olive oil	30 mL
2	garlic cloves, peeled and sliced	2
3	tomatoes, peeled, seeded and chopped	3
1 tsp	basil	5 mL
1	bay leaf	1
1 cup	chicken stock, heated	250 mL
	salt and pepper	

1 Remove stems and green leaves from fennel bulb. Cut in half and core. Slice thinly and set aside.

2 Cut chicken legs in half at the joint, between the thigh and the drumstick. Remove skin.

3 Heat oil in sauté pan over medium heat. Add chicken and cook 6 minutes on each side.

4 Add garlic and cook 1 minute. Add tomatoes and seasonings; cook 5 minutes over low heat.

5 Add sliced fennel and chicken stock. Cover and cook 20 minutes over low heat.

6 Remove chicken from pan and set aside.

7 Continue cooking, uncovered, 5 to 6 minutes. Sauce should be thick and fennel completely cooked.

8 Return chicken to pan and simmer 2 minutes. Serve with pasta and broccoli, if desired.

Chicken with Root Vegetables
(4 servings)

2	carrots, pared and cut in sticks	2
1/2	turnip, peeled and cut in sticks	1/2
3 1/2 lb	cleaned chicken, cut in 6 pieces	1.6 kg
2 tbsp	olive oil	30 mL
24	pearl onions, peeled	24
1 tsp	grated lemon zest	5 mL
1 tbsp	chopped fresh parsley	15 mL
1/4 tsp	thyme	1 mL
1/2 tsp	celery seeds	2 mL
1 1/2 cups	chicken stock, heated	375 mL
1 tbsp	cornstarch	15 mL
3 tbsp	cold water	45 mL
	salt and pepper	

1 Place carrots and turnip in salted, boiling water. Cook until vegetables are crisply tender. Cool under cold water, drain well and set aside.

2 Skin chicken pieces and season well. Heat oil in sauté pan over medium heat. Add chicken. Cook 18 minutes over low heat, turning pieces over 2 to 3 times.

3 Remove chicken breasts from pan and set aside.

4 Add cooked vegetables, pearl onions, lemon zest and all seasonings to pan with remaining chicken. Mix and continue cooking 10 minutes.

5 Return chicken breasts to pan. Cook 2 to 3 minutes over low heat.

6 Remove chicken pieces and keep warm on serving platter.

7 Increase heat to high and pour in chicken stock. Cook 4 minutes.

8 Dilute cornstarch in cold water; stir into sauce. Continue cooking 1 minute, then spoon over chicken. Serve with potatoes, if desired.

Chicken Breasts with Mixed Vegetables

(4 servings)

2	whole boneless chicken breasts	2
3 tbsp	butter	45 mL
2	shallots, peeled and sliced	2
1	cucumber, peeled, seeded and sliced ½ in (1 cm) thick	1
½ cup	sliced water chestnuts	125 mL
3 tbsp	sherry wine	45 mL
2 cups	chicken stock, heated	500 mL
2 tbsp	chopped fresh fennel	30 mL
1 tbsp	cornstarch	15 mL
3 tbsp	cold water	45 mL
	salt and pepper	

1 Skin chicken breasts and split in half. Season well. Heat butter in sauté pan over medium heat. Add chicken and cook 4 to 5 minutes on each side or adjust time according to size.

2 When cooked, remove chicken and set aside.

3 Add shallots, cucumber and water chestnuts to hot pan. Cook 2 minutes. Increase heat to high and pour in wine; cook 1 minute.

4 Add chicken stock and fennel; season well. Continue cooking 2 minutes.

5 Dilute cornstarch in cold water. Stir into sauce and cook 1 minute over low heat.

6 Return chicken to pan and simmer 3 minutes before serving. Accompany with potatoes and green beans, if desired.

Chicken Sauté with Mushroom Wine Sauce
(4 servings)

3 ½ lb	cleaned chicken, cut in 6 pieces	1.6 kg
1 tbsp	olive oil	15 mL
2 tbsp	butter	30 mL
12	shallots, peeled	12
½ lb	fresh mushrooms, cleaned and halved	225 g
1 tbsp	chopped fresh parsley	15 mL
1 tbsp	chopped fresh basil	15 mL
2 tbsp	flour	30 mL
1 cup	dry white wine	250 mL
	chicken stock, heated	125 mL
	salt and pepper	

1 Skin chicken pieces and season well. Heat oil and butter in sauté pan over medium heat. Add chicken and shallots. Cook 18 minutes over low heat, turning pieces over 2 to 3 times.

2 Remove chicken breasts from pan and set aside.

3 Add mushrooms and seasonings to sauté pan with remaining chicken. Cook 4 minutes over medium heat.

4 Sprinkle in flour and mix well. Pour in wine and chicken stock; mix again. Cook 6 minutes over low heat.

5 Return chicken breasts to pan and simmer 3 to 4 minutes over low heat before serving. Accompany with pasta and zucchini, if desired.

Roast Chicken with Fig Stuffing
(4 to 6 servings)

1/4 cup	butter	50 mL
6	shallots, peeled and quartered	6
1/2	celery stalk, diced	1/2
12	fresh figs, peeled and coarsely chopped	12
1	garlic clove, peeled and sliced	1
1/2 tsp	marjoram	2 mL
1 cup	long grain rice, rinsed	250 mL
2 cups	chicken stock, heated	500 mL
4 lb	chicken	1.8 kg
	salt and pepper	

Preheat oven to 425°F (220°C).

1 Heat 1 tbsp (15 mL) butter in saucepan over medium heat. Add shallots, celery and figs; cook 3 minutes.

2 Add garlic and marjoram. Stir and cook 1 minute. Add rice and mix well; cook 2 minutes.

3 Pour in chicken stock, season well and bring to boil. Cover and cook 20 minutes over very low heat.

4 Clean chicken and dry thoroughly. Season inside and out. Fill with fig stuffing and truss for roasting.

5 Place chicken in buttered roasting pan. Spread remaining butter over skin. Cook 20 minutes in oven.

6 Reduce heat to 350°F (180°C). Continue cooking chicken 1¼ hours or adjust time according to size, basting every 10 minutes.

7 Serve with a sauce, if desired.

Chicken and Mushrooms in Creamy Port Sauce
(4 servings)

2	whole boneless chicken breasts	2
4 tbsp	butter	60 mL
1 lb	fresh mushrooms, cleaned and cut in thirds	450 g
2	shallots, peeled and chopped	2
¼ cup	Port wine	50 mL
1 ¼ cups	heavy cream	300 mL
1 tbsp	chopped fresh basil	15 mL
	salt and pepper	

1 Skin chicken and cut in strips about ½ in (1 cm) wide. Heat half of butter in large frying pan over medium heat. Add half of chicken and season well. Cook 3 to 4 minutes over high heat, turning chicken over once. Remove chicken and set aside.

2 Add remaining chicken to hot pan and repeat cooking process. Set aside with first batch of cooked chicken.

3 Add remaining butter to pan. When hot, cook mushrooms and shallots 6 minutes over medium heat; season well.

4 Pour in Port wine and continue cooking 2 minutes. Mix in heavy cream, season and cook 4 minutes.

5 Return chicken to pan, mix and sprinkle with basil. Simmer 2 minutes over low heat and serve. Accompany with rice, green beans and sliced yellow zucchini, if desired.

Skin chicken and cut in strips about ½ in (1 cm) wide.

Add remaining chicken to hot pan and repeat cooking process. Set aside with first batch of cooked chicken.

Add remaining butter to pan. When hot, cook mushrooms and shallots 6 minutes over medium heat; season well.

Return chicken to pan, mix and sprinkle with basil. Simmer 2 minutes over low heat and serve.

Chicken Cacciatore
(4 servings)

3½ lb	cleaned chicken, cut in 6 pieces	1.6 kg
2 tbsp	olive oil	30 mL
3	garlic cloves, peeled and thinly sliced	3
2	shallots, peeled and chopped	2
½ lb	fresh mushrooms, cleaned and halved	225 g
½ cup	Chianti wine	125 mL
3	tomatoes, peeled, seeded and chopped	3
¼ tsp	chili powder	1 mL
1 tbsp	chopped fresh basil	15 mL
	salt and pepper	

1 Skin chicken pieces and season well. Heat oil in sauté pan over medium heat. Add chicken. Cook 18 minutes over low heat, turning pieces over 2 to 3 times.

2 Remove chicken breasts from pan and set aside.

3 Add garlic, shallots and mushrooms to pan with remaining chicken; season well. Cook 10 minutes over low heat.

4 Remove remaining chicken pieces from pan and set aside.

5 Increase heat under sauté pan to high. Pour in wine and cook 2 minutes. Add tomatoes, chili powder and basil; cook 6 minutes over medium heat.

6 Return chicken pieces to sauce in pan and simmer 3 minutes before serving. Accompany with pasta and broccoli, if desired.

Chicken with Cucumber
(4 servings)

3½ lb	cleaned chicken, cut in 6 pieces	1.6 kg
2 tbsp	olive oil	30 mL
1 tbsp	butter	15 mL
2	shallots, peeled and chopped	2
1	large cucumber, peeled, seeded and diced	1
2 tbsp	flour	30 mL
1 cup	dry white wine	250 mL
1 cup	chicken stock, heated	250 mL
1 tbsp	chopped fresh parsley	15 mL
	salt and pepper	
	few drops lemon juice	

1 Skin chicken pieces and season well. Heat oil and butter in sauté pan over medium heat. Add chicken. Cook 18 minutes over low heat, turning pieces over 2 to 3 times.

2 Remove chicken breasts from pan and set aside.

3 Add shallots and cucumber to pan with remaining chicken; cook 1 minute. Sprinkle in flour and mix well. Pour in wine and chicken stock; mix again. Cook 8 minutes over low heat.

4 Return chicken breasts to pan and continue cooking 3 minutes. Sprinkle with parsley and few drops of lemon juice. Serve with rice and eggplant, if desired.

Chicken with Bell Peppers and Tomatoes
(4 servings)

3½ lb	cleaned chicken, cut in 6 pieces	1.6 kg
3 tbsp	olive oil	45 mL
1	small onion, peeled and chopped	1
2	garlic cloves, peeled, crushed and chopped	2
1	chili pepper, seeded and chopped	1
1	green bell pepper, sliced	1
½	yellow bell pepper, sliced	½
½ cup	dry white wine	125 mL
2	tomatoes, peeled, seeded and coarsely chopped	2
1 tbsp	chopped fresh basil	15 mL
	salt and pepper	

1 Skin chicken pieces and season well. Heat oil in sauté pan over medium heat. Add chicken. Cook 18 minutes over low heat, turning pieces over 2 to 3 times.

2 Remove chicken breasts from pan and set aside.

3 Add onion, garlic, chili pepper and bell peppers to pan with remaining chicken. Cook 3 minutes over low heat. Pour in wine and cook 1 minute.

4 Add tomatoes and basil; season well. Cook 6 minutes over low heat.

5 Return chicken breasts to pan and cook another 3 to 4 minutes. Serve with fried potato cubes, if desired.

Chicken with Madeira Wine
(4 servings)

3½ lb	cleaned chicken, cut in 6 pieces	1.6 kg
2 tbsp	olive oil	30 mL
12	shallots, peeled	12
24	Parisienne potatoes, cooked 6 minutes	24
2	garlic cloves, peeled, crushed and chopped	2
4	artichoke bottoms, halved	4
¼ cup	Madeira wine	50 mL
1 tbsp	chopped fresh parsley	15 mL
	salt and pepper	

1 Skin chicken pieces and season well. Heat oil in sauté pan over medium heat. Add chicken. Cook 10 minutes over low heat, turning pieces over once or twice.

2 Add shallots and continue cooking 8 minutes.

3 Remove chicken breasts from pan and set aside.

4 Add Parisienne potatoes, garlic and artichoke bottoms to pan with remaining chicken; season well. Continue cooking 8 minutes over low heat.

5 Return chicken breasts to pan. Pour in wine and cook 4 minutes. Sprinkle chicken with parsley. Serve with asparagus, if desired.

Chicken Fricassée
(4 servings)

6 tbsp	olive oil	90 mL
4	½-in (1-cm) thick slices French bread, diced large	4
3	garlic cloves, peeled, crushed and chopped	3
3½ lb	cleaned chicken, cut in 8 pieces	1.6 kg
1 tbsp	butter	15 mL
24	pearl onions, peeled	24
½ lb	fresh mushroom caps, cleaned	225 g
½ cup	dry white wine	125 mL
1 cup	chicken stock, heated	250 mL
1 tbsp	cornstarch	15 mL
3 tbsp	cold water	45 mL
1 tbsp	chopped Italian parsley	15 mL
	salt and pepper	

1 Heat 4 tbsp (60 mL) oil in frying pan over high heat. Add bread and cook 2 minutes, browning on both sides. Add garlic; continue cooking 1 to 2 minutes over medium heat, stirring frequently. Transfer croutons to paper towel to drain.

2 Skin chicken pieces and season well. Heat butter and 2 tbsp (30 mL) oil in sauté pan over medium heat. Add chicken; cook 14 minutes over low heat, turning pieces over 2 to 3 times. Remove chicken breasts from pan and set aside.

3 Add pearl onions and mushroom caps to pan with remaining chicken; season well. Continue cooking 10 minutes over low heat.

4 Return chicken breasts to pan; simmer 4 minutes. Transfer chicken and vegetables to serving platter; keep warm.

5 Add wine to sauce remaining in pan. Increase heat to high and cook 2 minutes. Pour in chicken stock and cook 3 minutes.

6 Dilute cornstarch in cold water; stir into pan. Cook 1 minute, then pour sauce over chicken and vegetables. Sprinkle with parsley, add croutons and serve. Accompany with pasta, if desired.

Heat 4 tbsp (60 mL) oil in frying pan over high heat. Add diced bread and cook 2 minutes, browning bread on both sides. Add garlic and continue cooking 1 to 2 minutes over medium heat, stirring frequently.

Heat butter and 2 tbsp (30 mL) oil in sauté pan over medium heat. Add chicken; cook 14 minutes over low heat, turning pieces over 2 to 3 times.

Add pearl onions and mushroom caps to pan with remaining chicken; season well. Continue cooking 10 minutes over low heat.

Dilute cornstarch in cold water; stir into pan. Cook 1 minute.

Chicken with Tarragon Cream Sauce
(4 servings)

3½ lb	cleaned chicken, cut in 6 pieces	1.6 kg
3 tbsp	butter	45 mL
¾ lb	fresh mushrooms, cleaned and thickly sliced	350 g
¼ cup	coarsely chopped fresh tarragon	50 mL
1 cup	dry white wine	250 mL
1 cup	heavy cream	250 mL
	salt and pepper	
	cayenne pepper to taste	

1 Skin chicken pieces and season well with salt, pepper and cayenne pepper. Heat butter in sauté pan over medium heat. Add chicken. Cook 18 minutes over low heat, turning pieces over 2 to 3 times.

2 Remove chicken breasts from pan and set aside in warm oven.

3 Add mushrooms and tarragon to pan with remaining chicken. Mix well and cook 10 minutes over low heat.

4 Return chicken breasts to pan. Simmer 3 minutes.

5 Remove all chicken from pan and set aside in warm oven.

6 Increase heat under sauté pan to high. Add wine and cook 3 to 4 minutes. Pour in cream, season well and continue cooking 6 minutes.

7 Serve sauce over chicken. Accompany with rice, julienned zucchini and baby corn, if desired.

Texas Chicken Bake
(4 servings)

3½ lb	cleaned chicken, cut in 6 pieces	1.6 kg
2 tbsp	vegetable oil	30 mL
1 cup	chili sauce	250 mL
¼ cup	chopped onion	50 mL
2	garlic cloves, peeled and sliced	2
1 tbsp	wine vinegar	15 mL
¼ tsp	crushed chilies	1 mL
¼ tsp	chili powder	1 mL
½ tsp	ground oregano	2 mL
1 tbsp	Worcestershire sauce	15 mL
	salt and pepper	

Preheat oven to 350°F (180°C).

1 Skin chicken pieces and season well. Heat oil in ovenproof sauté pan over medium heat. Add chicken and brown 4 minutes on each side. If too much fat remains in pan, discard some.

2 Mix remaining ingredients together in a saucepan. Cook until mixture is hot.

3 Pour sauce over chicken and season well. Cover and cook 15 minutes in oven.

4 Remove chicken breasts and keep warm.

5 Continue cooking remaining chicken 16 to 18 minutes or adjust time according to size.

6 Four minutes before end of cooking, return chicken breasts to pan. Remove cover and finish cooking. Serve with French fries and corn, if desired.

Chicken in Classic Red Wine Sauce
(4 servings)

3½ lb	cleaned chicken, cut in 6 pieces	1.6 kg
3 tbsp	olive oil	45 mL
3	shallots, peeled and chopped	3
2	garlic cloves, peeled, crushed and chopped	2
½ lb	fresh mushrooms, cleaned and halved	225 g
1½ cups	dry red wine	375 mL
2 tbsp	butter	30 mL
1 tbsp	flour	15 mL
	salt and pepper	

1 Skin chicken pieces and season well. Heat oil in sauté pan over medium heat. Add chicken. Cook 18 minutes over low heat, turning pieces over 2 to 3 times.

2 Remove chicken breasts from pan and keep warm.

3 Add shallots, garlic and mushrooms to pan with remaining chicken; season well. Mix and cook 10 minutes over medium heat.

4 Remove remaining chicken pieces from pan and keep warm.

5 Increase heat under sauté pan to high and pour in wine. Cook 3 minutes.

6 Mix butter with flour to make smooth paste. Add to sauce, whisking well to incorporate. Return chicken pieces to sauce in pan and simmer 4 minutes over low heat. Serve with zucchini and potatoes, if desired.

Easy Chicken Casserole

(4 servings)

3½ lb	cleaned chicken, cut in 6 pieces	1.6 kg
2 tbsp	olive oil	30 mL
8	shallots, peeled and chopped	8
2	garlic cloves, peeled, crushed and chopped	2
1	sprig fresh rosemary	1
1	sprig fresh sage	1
2	sprigs fresh parsley	2
1	bay leaf	1
3	large tomatoes, peeled, seeded and coarsely chopped	3
1 tbsp	lime juice	15 mL
	salt and pepper	
	chopped fresh parsley	

Preheat oven to 350°F (180°C).

1 Skin chicken pieces and season well. Heat oil in ovenproof sauté pan over medium heat. Add chicken and brown 3 minutes on each side.

2 Add shallots and garlic; continue cooking 1 minute.

3 Tie herb sprigs and bay leaf together in bundle. Add to pan along with tomatoes. Season well, cover and cook 16 minutes in oven.

4 Remove chicken breasts from pan and set aside; keep warm.

5 Continue cooking remaining chicken in oven 16 to 18 minutes or adjust time according to size. Eight minutes before chicken is cooked, stir in lime juice.

6 Return chicken breasts to pan; simmer 2 minutes over low heat.

7 Transfer chicken pieces to heated serving platter; keep warm.

8 Remove bundle of herbs from pan and discard. Cook contents of sauté pan over high heat for 3 minutes. Pour over chicken and sprinkle with parsley. Serve with pasta and a vegetable medley, if desired.

Chicken with Roasted Peppers

(4 servings)

1	red bell pepper	1
1	green bell pepper	1
1	yellow bell pepper	1
2	chili peppers	2
3 tbsp	olive oil	45 mL
3 ½ lb	cleaned chicken, cut in 8 pieces	1.6 kg
2	garlic cloves, peeled and sliced	2
3 tbsp	lime juice	45 mL
	salt and pepper	

1 Cut bell peppers and chili peppers in half and remove seeds. Oil skin and place cut-side-down on cookie sheet; broil 6 minutes in oven. Remove chili peppers from oven and let cool. Continue broiling bell peppers 6 to 8 minutes, turning peppers over once. Peel off skin, cut into cubes and set aside.

2 Preheat oven to 350°F (180°C).

3 Skin chicken pieces and season well. Heat remaining oil in oven-proof sauté pan over medium heat. Add chicken and cook 4 minutes on each side.

4 Add garlic and mix. Cover and cook 15 minutes in oven.

5 Remove chicken breasts from pan and set aside; keep warm.

6 Add roasted peppers to pan and continue cooking remaining chicken 12 minutes or adjust time according to size.

7 Return chicken breasts to pan and stir in lime juice. Finish cooking 3 minutes, then serve over rice.

Broiled Chicken Kebabs

(4 servings)

2	whole boneless chicken breasts	2
¼ cup	sake wine	50 mL
3 tbsp	soy sauce	45 mL
1 tsp	sesame oil	5 mL
2	garlic cloves, peeled and sliced	2
½ tsp	crushed chilies	2 mL
½ tsp	coriander seeds	2 mL
1 tsp	cumin	5 mL
1 tbsp	honey	15 mL
1 tsp	sesame seeds	5 mL
	juice of 1 lemon	
	freshly ground pepper	

1 Skin chicken and cut into pieces 1 in (2.5 cm) wide. Place in bowl.

2 Mix remaining ingredients, except sesame seeds, together and pour over chicken.

3 Mix well, cover and refrigerate chicken 1 hour.

4 Thread chicken pieces on metal skewers. Broil 6 to 8 minutes in oven or adjust time according to size. Baste with marinade and rotate skewers during cooking.

5 Sprinkle with sesame seeds and serve over rice. Accompany with snow peas, yellow bell pepper and mushrooms, if desired.

Burgundy Chicken
(4 servings)

4 lb	cleaned chicken, cut in 6 pieces	1.8 kg
1 tsp	olive oil	5 mL
¼ lb	bacon, diced	125 g
24	pearl onions, peeled	24
3	garlic cloves, peeled, crushed and chopped	3
½ lb	fresh mushroom caps, cleaned	225 g
3 cups	full bodied Californian red wine	750 mL
3	sprigs fresh parsley	3
1	sprig fresh thyme	1
2	bay leaves	2
2 tbsp	flour	30 mL
3 tbsp	butter	45 mL
	salt and pepper / pinch of sugar	

Preheat oven to 350°F (180°C).

1 Skin chicken pieces and season well. Heat oil in large ovenproof casserole. Add bacon and cook 4 minutes over low heat. Add onions and cook 4 minutes longer.

2 Using slotted spoon, remove bacon and onions; set aside. Add chicken pieces to hot pan. Brown 4 minutes on each side over low heat.

3 Return bacon and onions to pan. Add garlic and mushrooms; mix and cook 1 minute.

4 Add wine and pinch of sugar. Tie herb sprigs and bay leaves together in bundle. Add to pan and season well. Cover and cook 40 to 45 minutes in oven.

5 When chicken is cooked, remove from pan. Remove onions and mushrooms; set aside. Discard herbs.

6 Place pan on stove over high heat. Mix flour with butter to make paste. Add to sauce, mixing quickly with whisk. Cook 2 minutes.

7 Add chicken, onions and mushrooms to sauce. Simmer 3 minutes over low heat. Serve over noodles.

Chicken Schnitzel
(4 servings)

2	whole boneless chicken breasts	2
½ cup	grated Parmesan cheese	125 mL
2	eggs, beaten	2
1½ cups	breadcrumbs	375 mL
¼ cup	vegetable oil	50 mL
4	slices lemon, decorated with anchovy fillets	4
	salt and pepper	

1 Skin chicken, split into halves and remove fat. Using wooden mallet, flatten breasts between two sheets of waxed paper. Breasts should be about ¼ in (5 mm) thick.

2 Season chicken well and dredge in Parmesan cheese. Dip in beaten eggs, then coat thoroughly with breadcrumbs.

3 Heat oil in large frying pan over medium heat. Add chicken and cook 3 to 4 minutes on each side, or adjust time according to size.

4 Serve decorated with lemon slices and accompany with tomato sauce, if desired.

Chicken en Cocotte
(4 servings)

¼ lb	bacon, diced	125 g
24	pearl onions, peeled	24
3½ lb	cleaned chicken, trussed	1.6 kg
8	small new potatoes, peeled	8
2	large carrots, pared and cut in 1-in (2.5-cm) lengths	2
1½ cups	chicken stock, heated	375 mL
2	sprigs fresh parsley	2
1	sprig fresh thyme	1
1 tbsp	butter	15 mL
4	artichoke bottoms, halved	4
1 tbsp	cornstarch	15 mL
3 tbsp	cold water	45 mL
	salt and pepper	

Preheat oven to 325°F (160°C).

1 Place bacon in medium-size cocotte*. Cook 3 minutes over medium heat. Add onions and reduce heat to low; cook 3 minutes. Remove bacon and onions and set aside.

2 Place chicken in cocotte. Cook 16 minutes over low heat, browning on all sides.

3 Add potatoes and carrots; season well. Continue cooking 15 minutes. Pour in chicken stock, add fresh herbs and reserved bacon and onions. Cover and finish cooking 35 to 40 minutes in oven.

4 About 8 minutes before end of cooking, heat butter in frying pan over medium heat. Add artichoke bottoms and sauté 2 minutes. Add to chicken.

5 When chicken is cooked, transfer with vegetables to heated serving platter.

6 Place cocotte on stove over medium heat. Dilute cornstarch in cold water; stir into sauce. Cook 1 minute and accompany chicken with sauce.

*A cocotte is a deep oval casserole with a tight-fitting lid.

Place bacon in medium-size cocotte. Cook 3 minutes over medium heat. Add onions and reduce heat to low; cook 3 minutes.

Add potatoes and carrots; season well. Continue cooking 15 minutes.

Pour in chicken stock, add fresh herbs and reserved bacon and onions.

Add cooked artichoke bottoms to chicken.

Chicken with Garlic-Anchovy Purée
(4 servings)

12	anchovy fillets, rinsed and drained	12
6	garlic cloves, blanched and puréed	6
¼ cup	white wine vinegar	50 mL
¼ cup	dry white wine	50 mL
1 tbsp	chopped fresh basil	15 mL
2	whole boneless chicken breasts	2
4 tbsp	olive oil	60 mL
	freshly ground pepper	

1 Purée anchovy fillets and garlic in mortar. Incorporate vinegar, wine and basil to make paste. Set aside.

2 Skin chicken and cut into 1-in (2.5-cm) pieces. Heat 3 tbsp (45 mL) of oil in frying pan over high heat. When hot, add half of chicken pieces, season with pepper and stir-fry 2 to 3 minutes over high heat. Remove chicken from pan.

3 Add remaining chicken to hot pan and repeat cooking process. Set aside with first batch of chicken.

4 Add remaining oil to hot pan. Stir in anchovy purée and cook 30 seconds.

5 Return chicken to pan and mix well. Cook 1 minute and serve over rice. Accompany with cucumbers, if desired.

Breast of Chicken with Green Grapes
(4 servings)

2	**whole boneless chicken breasts**	2
3 tbsp	**butter**	45 mL
2	**shallots, peeled and sliced**	2
I tbsp	**honey**	15 mL
I cup	**dry white wine**	250 mL
I tsp	**tarragon**	5 mL
I ¼ cups	**seedless green grapes**	300 mL
½ cup	**heavy cream**	125 mL
	salt and pepper	
	chopped fresh parsley	

1 Skin chicken and split into halves. Heat butter in sauté over medium heat. Add chicken, season and cook 2 minutes on each side.

2 Add shallots and honey. Cook 8 to 10 minutes over low heat. Remove chicken and set aside; keep warm.

3 Add wine and tarragon to hot pan. Cook 2 minutes over high heat. Stir in green grapes and cream; season well. Cook 3 minutes over medium heat.

4 Return chicken to sauce in pan and simmer 1 minute. Sprinkle with chopped parsley and serve. Accompany with potatoes, if desired.

Boiled Chicken and Rice
(4 servings)

3	carrots, pared	3
2	celery stalks	2
2	bay leaves	2
3	sprigs fresh parsley	3
1	sprig fresh thyme	1
2	sprigs fresh basil	2
4 lb	cleaned chicken, trussed	1.8 kg
10 cups	water	2.5 L
2	onions, peeled and studded with cloves	2
1 ½ cups	long grain rice, rinsed	375 mL
	salt and pepper	

1 Tie carrots and celery together with bay leaves and fresh herbs.

2 Place chicken in large pot and pour in water. Bring to boil and cook over medium heat for 10 minutes. During this time, skim surface of water.

3 Add all vegetables and herbs to pot; season well. Cook 1½ hours, partly covered, over very low heat. The key to this recipe is the gentle cooking of the chicken: water should barely bubble. After 1 hour, add rice.

4 Serve chicken with rice.

Macaroni and Chicken Casserole
(4 to 6 servings)

4	large chicken legs	4
5 tbsp	butter	75 mL
1/2	celery stalk, diced	1/2
2	garlic cloves, peeled and sliced	2
2	shallots, peeled and chopped	2
1	bay leaf	1
1/4 tsp	thyme	1 mL
2 cups	chicken stock, heated	500 mL
4 tbsp	flour	60 mL
2 cups	cooked macaroni	500 mL
1 1/2 cups	grated Gruyère cheese	375 mL
	salt and pepper	

Preheat oven to 375°F (190°C).

1 Cut chicken legs in half at the joint, between the thigh and the drumstick. Remove skin and bones. Cut meat into 1-in (2.5-cm) pieces.

2 Heat 1 tbsp (15 mL) butter in frying pan over medium heat. Add chicken, celery, garlic and shallots; season well. Cook 3 minutes.

3 Add bay leaf, thyme and chicken stock. Cover and cook 8 to 10 minutes over low heat. When meat is well cooked, remove from pan with slotted spoon. Reserve cooking liquid; discard vegetables.

4 Heat remaining butter in saucepan over medium heat. Mix in flour and cook 1 minute.

5 Incorporate reserved cooking liquid, mixing well with whisk. Correct seasoning and cook sauce 5 minutes over low heat, stirring occasionally.

6 To assemble casserole, place layer of cooked macaroni in buttered baking dish. Add layers of chicken, sauce and cheese. Repeat all layers, ending with cheese.

7 Bake 12 minutes in oven and serve with crusty bread.

Peasant Chicken
(4 servings)

3½ lb	cleaned chicken, cut in 6 pieces	1.6 kg
3 tbsp	butter	45 mL
2	leeks, white part only	2
4	artichoke bottoms, cut in thirds	4
½ cup	dry white wine	125 mL
1 cup	heavy cream	250 mL
1 tbsp	chopped fresh parsley	15 mL
	salt and pepper	
	cayenne pepper to taste	

1 Skin chicken pieces and season well with salt, pepper and cayenne pepper. Heat butter in sauté pan over medium heat. Add chicken. Cook 8 minutes over low heat, turning pieces over once.

2 Meanwhile, prepare leeks for cooking. Slit leeks from top to bottom twice, leaving 1 in (2.5 cm) intact at base. Wash leeks under cold, running water to remove dirt and sand. Drain and slice.

3 Add leeks to pan and continue cooking 10 minutes over low heat. Turn chicken pieces over once.

4 Remove chicken breasts from pan and set aside.

5 Add artichoke bottoms and wine to pan with remaining chicken; cook 4 minutes. Add cream and season well; cook 6 minutes over low heat.

6 Return chicken breasts to pan and simmer 3 minutes. Sprinkle with parsley and serve. Accompany with rice, if desired.

Chicken Marsala
(4 servings)

4	**chicken legs**	4
1 tbsp	**butter**	15 mL
2 tbsp	**olive oil**	30 mL
2	**leeks, white part only, cleaned and chopped**	2
¹/₂ cup	**Marsala wine**	125 mL
1 ¹/₂ cups	**chicken stock, heated**	375 mL
¹/₄ tsp	**thyme**	1 mL
¹/₂ lb	**fresh mushroom caps, cleaned**	225 g
1 tbsp	**cornstarch**	15 mL
3 tbsp	**cold water**	45 mL
	salt and pepper	
	pinch of sage	

1 Cut chicken legs in half at the joint, between the thigh and the drumstick. Remove skin.

2 Heat butter and half of oil in sauté pan over medium heat. Add chicken and cook 6 minutes on each side.

3 Add leeks and continue cooking 4 minutes. Pour in wine and cook 2 minutes.

4 Add chicken stock and seasonings. Cover and cook 20 minutes over low heat, stirring once during cooking.

5 Heat remaining oil in frying pan over high heat. Cook mushroom caps 5 minutes.

6 Add mushrooms to chicken in pan. Cook 4 minutes, then remove chicken and set aside.

7 Dilute cornstarch in cold water; stir into sauce. Cook 1 minute. Return chicken to pan, simmer 1 minute and serve. Accompany with pasta and snow peas, if desired.

Roasted Chicken Pieces

(4 servings)

3½ lb	cleaned chicken, cut in 6 pieces	1.6 kg
3 tbsp	melted butter	45 mL
	Seasoned Rub (see page 94)	
	salt and pepper	

Preheat oven to 400°F (200°C). Preheat broiling rack.

1 Skin chicken pieces and score flesh.

2 Mix seasoned rub with melted butter. Rub into scored chicken and refrigerate pieces 1 hour.

3 Season chicken with salt and pepper. Place directly on preheated broiling rack and cook 18 minutes in oven.

4 Remove chicken breasts and set aside; keep warm.

5 Reduce oven heat to 350°F (180°C). Continue cooking remaining chicken 15 to 20 minutes or adjust time according to size.

6 Reheat chicken breasts briefly. Serve roasted chicken pieces with green salad.

Devil Chicken
(4 servings)

2	2½-lb (1.2-kg) cleaned chickens	2
¼ tsp	oregano powder	1 mL
¼ tsp	chili powder	1 mL
¼ tsp	sage powder	1 mL
¼ cup	melted butter	50 mL
½ cup	breadcrumbs	125 mL
	pinch of cayenne pepper / salt	

Preheat oven to 350°F (180°C).

1 Using poultry shears, cut chickens in half. Make a small incision in thigh flesh to tuck in drumstick. Snip the wing tendon to prevent leg from springing out during cooking.

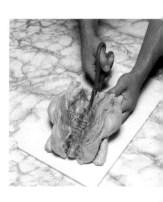

2 Mix all seasonings together. Brush chicken with some of melted butter, then sprinkle with seasonings.

3 Change oven setting to broil. Place chicken halves in roasting pan, skin-side-up. Place in oven, 6 in (15 cm) from top element. Cook 15 minutes, basting frequently.

4 Turn chicken over, season with salt and continue cooking 15 minutes, basting frequently.

5 Change oven setting back to roast and cook chicken another 30 minutes or adjust time according to size, turning halves over twice. Baste frequently.

6 Test if chicken is done by inserting metal skewer in thigh. Juices should run clear.

7 About 6 minutes before chicken is cooked, brush with remaining melted butter and cover with breadcrumbs.

Chicken Beaulieu
(4 servings)

3½ lb	cleaned chicken, cut in 6 pieces	1.6 kg
3 tbsp	olive oil	45 mL
½ cup	pitted black olives	125 mL
4	artichoke bottoms, sliced in thirds	4
1	garlic clove, peeled, crushed and chopped	1
2	tomatoes, peeled, seeded and coarsely chopped	2
1 cup	dry white wine	250 mL
	salt and pepper	
	lemon juice to taste	

1 Skin chicken pieces and season well. Heat oil in sauté pan over medium heat. Add chicken and cook 18 minutes over low heat, turning pieces over 2 to 3 times.

2 Remove chicken breasts from pan and set aside.

3 Add olives, artichoke bottoms and garlic to pan with remaining chicken. Cook 2 minutes. Stir in tomatoes and continue cooking 8 minutes.

4 Return chicken breasts to pan and simmer 3 minutes. Season well and remove all chicken pieces; keep warm.

5 Add wine to sauce remaining in pan. Cook 3 minutes over high heat. Add lemon juice to taste, cook 2 minutes and pour over chicken. Serve with potatoes and green beans, if desired.

Spicy Worcestershire Chicken Strips
(4 servings)

2	**whole boneless chicken breasts**	2
¼ cup	**olive oil**	50 mL
5	**green onions, cut in 1-in (2.5-cm) lengths**	5
4	**shallots, peeled and sliced**	4
24	**cherry tomatoes, halved**	24
2	**red bell peppers, thinly sliced**	2
3	**garlic cloves, peeled and sliced**	3
2 tbsp	**Worcestershire sauce**	30 mL
	salt and pepper	

1 Skin chicken and cut in strips about ½ in (1 cm) wide. Heat half of oil in large frying pan over high heat. Add chicken and season well. Cook 3 to 4 minutes over high heat, turning chicken over once.

2 Remove chicken from pan and set aside.

3 Add remaining oil to pan. When hot, add vegetables and garlic; season well. Cook 3 minutes over high heat.

4 Return chicken to pan. Add Worcestershire sauce, mix and cook 1 minute. Serve with rice, if desired.

Breast of Chicken à la Parisienne
(4 servings)

2	whole boneless chicken breasts	2
3 tbsp	butter	45 mL
2	shallots, peeled and chopped	2
1	large carrot, pared and thinly sliced	1
1/2 lb	fresh mushrooms, cleaned and diced	225 g
2	garlic cloves, peeled and sliced	2
1/2 cup	dry white wine	125 mL
1 1/4 cups	chicken stock, heated	300 mL
1 tbsp	cornstarch	15 mL
3 tbsp	cold water	45 mL
	salt and pepper	

1 Skin chicken and split into halves. Season with salt and pepper. Heat half of butter in sauté pan over medium heat. Add chicken and cook 8 to 10 minutes or adjust time according to size. Turn breasts over halfway through cooking.

2 Remove chicken from pan and keep warm.

3 Add remaining butter to pan. Add shallots, carrot and mushrooms; season well. Add garlic and cook 3 minutes over high heat.

4 Pour in wine and continue cooking 2 minutes. Add chicken stock, reduce heat to low and cook 3 minutes.

5 Dilute cornstarch in cold water. Stir into sauce, mixing well. Return chicken to pan and simmer 3 minutes. Serve with potatoes, if desired.

Sweet and Sour Drumsticks

(4 servings)

12	chicken drumsticks	12
3 tbsp	soy sauce	45 mL
2 tbsp	teriyaki sauce	30 mL
3	garlic cloves, peeled and sliced	3
1 tbsp	chopped fresh ginger	15 mL
¼ tsp	coriander	1 mL
4 tbsp	honey	60 mL
	salt and pepper	

1 Leave skin on drumsticks, season and place in bowl.

2 Place remaining ingredients in small saucepan. Cook 3 minutes over medium heat, then pour over chicken. Mix and refrigerate 1 hour.

3 Preheat oven to 350°F (180°C).

4 Transfer drumsticks to baking dish. Cook 40 to 45 minutes in oven for medium-size drumsticks or adjust time according to size. Baste with marinade during cooking.

5 When cooked, change oven setting to broil. Brown several minutes and serve with your choice of vegetables.

Chicken and Shrimp Sauté
(4 servings)

3½ lb	cleaned chicken, cut in 6 pieces	1.6 kg
2 tbsp	olive oil	30 mL
6	garlic cloves, peeled	6
½ lb	fresh mushrooms, cleaned and halved	225 g
1 tbsp	chopped fresh tarragon	15 mL
½ lb	fresh shrimp, peeled and deveined	225 g
½ cup	dry white wine	125 mL
1 tbsp	chopped fresh basil	15 mL
	salt and pepper	

1 Skin chicken pieces and season well. Heat oil in sauté pan over medium heat. Add chicken and garlic. Cook 18 minutes over low heat, turning chicken pieces over 2 to 3 times.

2 Remove chicken breasts from pan and set aside in warm oven.

3 Add mushrooms and tarragon to pan. Continue cooking 6 minutes.

4 Increase heat to medium. Add shrimp and cook 4 minutes. Season and mix well.

5 Transfer the shrimp and remaining chicken pieces to chicken breasts, keeping warm in oven.

6 Increase heat under sauté pan to high. Pour in wine and cook 3 minutes. Pour sauce over shrimp and chicken and sprinkle with fresh basil. Serve with rice, if desired.

Chicken Lyonnaise
(4 servings)

3½ lb	cleaned chicken, cut in 6 pieces	1.6 kg
3 tbsp	olive oil	45 mL
3	onions, peeled and thinly sliced	3
1 cup	chicken stock, heated	250 mL
1 tbsp	chopped fresh parsley	15 mL
	salt and pepper	

1 Skin chicken pieces and season well. Heat oil in sauté pan over medium heat. Add chicken. Cook 10 minutes over low heat, turning pieces over once.

2 Add onions and turn chicken pieces again. Continue cooking 8 minutes over low heat.

3 Remove chicken breasts from pan and set aside in warm oven. Continue cooking remaining chicken and onions 10 minutes.

4 Remove remaining chicken from pan and set aside with chicken breasts.

5 Continue cooking onions in pan another 8 minutes or until completely cooked. Onions must be soft.

6 Pour in chicken stock and cook 2 minutes over medium heat. Sprinkle with chopped parsley and serve onions over chicken. Accompany with carrots, potatoes and spinach, if desired.

Chicken with Curry and Tomatoes
(4 servings)

3½ lb	cleaned chicken, cut in 8 pieces	1.6 kg
3 tbsp	olive oil	45 mL
2	onions, peeled and chopped	2
2	garlic cloves, peeled, crushed and chopped	2
2 tbsp	curry powder	30 mL
3	tomatoes, peeled, seeded and chopped	3
	salt and pepper	

1 Skin chicken pieces and season well. Heat oil in sauté pan over medium heat. Add chicken, onions and garlic. Cook 4 minutes over low heat. Do not allow onions to burn.

2 Mix in curry powder. Continue cooking 4 minutes. Add tomatoes, season and cook another 8 minutes over low heat.

3 Remove chicken breasts from pan and set aside.

4 Continue cooking remaining chicken in pan 10 to 12 minutes over low heat.

5 Return chicken breasts to pan, cook 4 minutes, and serve over rice.

Chicken Legs with Sauerkraut
(4 servings)

4	chicken legs	4
¼ cup	butter	50 mL
1	onion, peeled and chopped	1
2	garlic cloves, peeled	2
2 lb	fresh sauerkraut	900 g
1	large apple, cored, peeled and diced	1
1 cup	dry white wine	250 mL
1 cup	chicken stock, heated	250 mL
1	bay leaf	1
	salt and pepper	
	pinch of each: thyme, caraway seeds, juniper berries	

Preheat oven to 350°F (180°C).

1 Cut chicken legs in half at the joint, between the thigh and the drumstick. Remove skin.

2 Heat half of butter in frying pan over medium heat. Add chicken and season well. Cook 6 minutes on each side. Remove chicken and set aside.

3 Heat remaining butter in ovenproof casserole over medium heat. Add onion and garlic; cook 3 minutes. Add sauerkraut and cook 8 minutes.

4 Mix in remaining ingredients and bring to boil. Cover and cook 45 minutes in oven.

5 Add seared chicken to sauerkraut. If more liquid is needed, add more chicken stock. Cover and finish cooking 45 minutes in oven.

6 Serve chicken on bed of sauerkraut. Accompany with beets, if desired.

Chicken Meatballs
(4 servings)

1 ½ lb	ground chicken	700 g
3	garlic cloves, blanched and puréed	3
2 tbsp	breadcrumbs	30 mL
1 tsp	curry powder	5 mL
1	small egg, beaten	1
3 tbsp	olive oil	45 mL
2	bell peppers, sliced	2
4	tomatoes, peeled, seeded and chopped	4
1 tbsp	chopped fresh basil	15 mL
¼ tsp	grated lemon zest	1 mL
	salt and pepper	
	cayenne pepper to taste	

1 Place ground chicken, garlic, breadcrumbs and curry powder in food processor. Blend briefly. Season well with salt, pepper and cayenne pepper. Add beaten egg. Blend again until mixture takes shape and starts to form ball.

2 Shape mixture by hand into small meatballs, cover and refrigerate 15 minutes or until firm.

3 Heat half of oil in sauté pan over medium heat. Add meatballs and cook 4 to 5 minutes, browning on all sides. When cooked, remove meatballs and set aside to drain on paper towel.

4 Add remaining oil to pan if needed. Cook sliced bell peppers 3 minutes. Remove peppers and set aside.

5 Add chopped tomatoes, basil and lemon zest; season well. Cook 12 minutes over medium heat. Return sliced peppers and meatballs to pan. Simmer 3 minutes, then serve over pasta.

Place ground chicken, garlic, breadcrumbs and curry powder in food processor. Blend briefly. Season well with salt, pepper and cayenne pepper. Add beaten egg.

Shape mixture by hand into small meatballs.

Heat half of oil in sauté pan over medium heat. Add meatballs and cook 4 to 5 minutes, browning on all sides.

Add chopped tomatoes, basil and lemon zest; season well. Cook 12 minutes over medium heat. Return sliced peppers and meatballs to pan.

Basic Poached Chicken Breasts
(4 servings)

2	whole boneless chicken breasts	2
1/2	celery stalk, sliced	1/2
1	carrot, pared and sliced	1
5	fresh basil leaves	5
4	shallots, peeled	4
1	sprig fresh thyme	1
2	sprigs fresh parsley	2
	salt and pepper	

1 Skin chicken and split into halves. Trim off all fat and rinse chicken under cold water.

2 Place chicken breasts in sauté pan. Add remaining ingredients, seasoning well. Pour in enough cold water to cover; bring to boil.

3 Reduce heat and cook over low heat 8 to 10 minutes or adjust time according to size. Water should simmer.

4 When cooked, remove chicken from pan. If using liquid for a sauce, boil 2 to 3 minutes over high heat to bring out flavors.

Note: This method of cooking is ideal for chicken used in sandwiches, chicken pot pie or chicken salads.

Poached Chicken Breasts with Fresh Spinach
(4 servings)

2	bunches fresh spinach, well cleaned	2
2	whole boneless chicken breasts	2
1/2	celery stalk, diced	1/2
1	carrot, pared and sliced	1
1	onion, peeled and quartered	1
1	bay leaf	1
2 1/2 cups	water	625 mL
4 tbsp	butter	60 mL
3 tbsp	flour	45 mL
1	garlic clove, peeled and sliced	1
1 tbsp	chopped fresh basil	15 mL
1/2 cup	grated Gruyère cheese	125 mL
	salt and pepper	

Preheat oven to 350°F (180°C).

1 Steam spinach, drain well and chop. Set aside.

2 Skin chicken and split into halves. Place in sauté pan with celery, carrot and onion. Add bay leaf and season well. Pour in water and bring to boil over medium-high heat. Reduce heat to low and simmer 10 minutes.

3 Remove chicken from pan and set aside. Continue cooking liquid 5 minutes over high heat. Strain cooking liquid into bowl; set aside.

4 Heat 2 tbsp (30 mL) butter in saucepan. When melted, sprinkle in flour and mix well; cook 1 minute over low heat. Pour in strained cooking liquid, whisking to incorporate. Season and cook sauce 12 minutes over low heat.

5 Meanwhile, heat remaining butter in frying pan over medium heat. Add garlic and cook 1 minute. Add chopped spinach and basil; cook 3 minutes over medium heat.

6 Transfer spinach to baking dish. Place chicken breasts on spinach and pour in sauce. Top with grated cheese. Bake 8 minutes. Serve with potatoes and carrots, if desired.

Baked Chicken with Chives and Cream
(4 servings)

3½ lb	cleaned chicken, cut in 6 pieces	1.6 kg
2 tbsp	butter	30 mL
1 tbsp	olive oil	15 mL
1	red onion, peeled and sliced in rings	1
½ lb	fresh mushroom caps, cleaned	225 g
¾ cup	dry white wine	175 mL
2 tbsp	chopped fresh chives	30 mL
¼ cup	heavy cream	50 mL
	salt and pepper	

Preheat oven to 350°F (180°C).

1 Skin chicken pieces and season well. Heat butter and oil in oven-proof sauté pan over medium heat. Add chicken and cook 2 minutes on each side.

2 Add onion and stir. Cover and cook 18 minutes in oven.

3 Remove chicken breasts from pan and set aside; keep warm.

4 Add mushrooms, season and continue cooking with remaining chicken in oven 10 to 12 minutes.

5 Remove remaining chicken from pan and keep warm. Place pan on stove over high heat. Pour in wine and cook 4 minutes. Do not cover.

6 Stir in chives and cream; season well. Continue cooking 3 minutes over high heat.

7 Reduce heat to low. Return all chicken to pan and simmer 3 minutes. Serve with beets, if desired.

Chicken, Cucumber and Pearl Onions
(4 servings)

3½ lb	cleaned chicken, cut in 6 pieces	1.6 kg
3 tbsp	butter	45 mL
24	pearl onions, peeled and blanched	24
1	large cucumber, peeled, seeded and cut in ½-in (1-cm) pieces	1
1 tbsp	chopped fresh basil	15 mL
1 tbsp	chopped fresh parsley	15 mL
	salt and pepper	
	juice of 1 lemon	

1 Skin chicken pieces and season well. Heat butter in sauté pan over medium heat. Add chicken. Cook 18 minutes over low heat, turning pieces over 2 to 3 times.

2 Remove chicken breasts from pan and set aside.

3 Add pearl onions to pan with remaining chicken and cook 4 minutes. Add cucumber and herbs; season well. Cook 6 minutes over low heat.

4 Return chicken breasts to pan and add lemon juice. Simmer 3 minutes before serving. Accompany with potatoes, if desired.

Chicken with Eggplant and Red Onion
(4 servings)

2	whole boneless chicken breasts	2
¼ cup	olive oil	50 mL
½	eggplant, sliced ¼ in (5 mm) thick	½
I	large red onion, peeled and sliced	I
I tbsp	chopped fresh basil	15 mL
I tbsp	chopped fresh parsley	15 mL
2	garlic cloves, peeled, crushed and chopped	2
I tbsp	soy sauce	15 mL
	salt and pepper	

1 Skin chicken and cut in strips about ½ in (I cm) wide. Set aside.

2 Heat half of oil in large frying pan over high heat. Add eggplant slices and cook 3 to 4 minutes on each side. Remove eggplant from pan and keep warm in oven.

3 Add onion rings to hot pan. Cook 3 to 4 minutes. Remove from pan and transfer to oven.

4 Add remaining oil to pan. When hot, add half of chicken and season well. Cook 3 to 4 minutes over high heat, turning chicken over once. Remove chicken and set aside.

5 Add remaining chicken to hot pan and repeat cooking process.

6 Return first batch of cooked chicken to pan. Add herbs and garlic; cook I minute. Sprinkle in soy sauce and mix well. Cook 30 seconds and serve with eggplant and onion. Accompany with polenta, if desired.

Szechuan Drumsticks
(4 servings)

12	chicken drumsticks	12
¼ cup	Szechuan sauce	50 mL
3	blanched garlic cloves, puréed	3
2 tbsp	sesame oil	30 mL
½ cup	dry white wine	125 mL
¼ tsp	ground cloves	1 mL
1 tbsp	celery seeds	15 mL
¼ cup	honey	50 mL
	salt and pepper	
	juice of ½ lemon	

1 Leave skin on drumsticks. Mix Szechuan sauce, garlic, oil, wine and seasonings in bowl. Place chicken in marinade and mix well. Refrigerate for at least 1 hour.

2 Preheat oven to 350°F (180°C).

3 Transfer drumsticks to baking dish. Cook 40 to 45 minutes in oven for medium size drumsticks or adjust time according to size.

4 Mix honey with lemon juice. When chicken is cooked, baste with mixture. Broil a few minutes, being careful not to burn honey, and serve. Accompany with julienned green bell pepper and cherry tomatoes, if desired.

Marinated Chicken Brochettes
(4 servings)

2 tbsp	lemon juice	30 mL
2 tbsp	balsamic vinegar	30 mL
2 tbsp	olive oil	30 mL
1 tsp	honey	5 mL
1/2 tsp	oregano	2 mL
1 1/2	whole boneless chicken breasts	1 1/2
1	red onion, peeled	1
1	green bell pepper	1
16	large mushroom caps, cleaned	16
	pinch of thyme	
	few drops of Tabasco sauce	
	salt and freshly ground pepper	

1 Place lemon juice, vinegar, oil, honey, oregano, thyme, Tabasco sauce, salt and pepper in large bowl.

2 Skin chicken and cut into pieces 1 in (2.5 cm) wide. Place in marinade, cover and refrigerate 1 hour.

3 Preheat oven to 350°F (180°C).

4 Cut red onion and green pepper into bite-size pieces suitable for skewering.

5 Alternate pieces of chicken, red onion, green pepper and mushrooms on metal skewers. Set on ovenproof tray and baste with some of marinade.

6 Change oven setting to broil. When hot, place skewers in oven and broil 8 minutes, rotating two or three times during cooking. If brochettes start to burn, transfer to lower oven rack.

7 Serve over rice.

Spicy Chicken Bites
(4 servings)

¼ cup	balsamic vinegar	50 mL
1	jalapeño pepper, seeded and chopped	1
2 tbsp	soy sauce	30 mL
1 tbsp	lemon juice	15 mL
1 tsp	English mustard	5 mL
1	garlic clove, peeled, crushed and chopped	1
1 tbsp	honey	15 mL
¼ tsp	thyme	1 mL
1 tsp	oregano	5 mL
2	whole boneless chicken breasts	2
1 cup	flour	250 mL
2	eggs, beaten	2
1 cup	breadcrumbs	250 mL
	salt and pepper	
	peanut oil for cooking	

1 Place vinegar, jalapeño pepper, soy sauce and lemon juice in large bowl. Mix in mustard, garlic, honey and seasonings.

2 Skin chicken and cut into pieces 1 in (2.5 cm) wide. Place in bowl and mix well. Cover and marinate 1 hour in refrigerator.

3 Dredge chicken pieces in flour. Dip in beaten eggs and roll in breadcrumbs.

4 Cook chicken pieces in hot oil 3 to 4 minutes. Drain on paper towel. Serve chicken bites with pineapple chunks, if desired.

Fast-Fry Seasoned Chicken Strips
(4 servings)

2	whole boneless chicken breasts	2
2 tbsp	olive oil	30 mL
3	garlic cloves, peeled, crushed and chopped	3
I tbsp	chopped fresh tarragon	15 mL
I tbsp	chopped fresh basil	15 mL
I tsp	chopped fresh parsley	5 mL
	salt and pepper	
	juice of I lemon	

1 Skin chicken and cut in strips about ¼ in (5 mm) wide. Heat oil in frying pan over medium heat. Add chicken, season well and cook 2 to 3 minutes.

2 Remove chicken from pan and set aside.

3 Add garlic and cook 1 minute. Add fresh herbs and return chicken to pan. Cook 30 seconds.

4 Sprinkle in lemon juice, toss well and serve at once over rice. Accompany with asparagus, if desired.

Marinated Chicken Legs
(4 servings)

¼ cup	olive oil	50 mL
2 tbsp	chili sauce	30 mL
1 cup	orange juice	250 mL
1 tbsp	chopped fresh basil	15 mL
½ tsp	thyme	2 mL
2	garlic cloves, peeled, crushed and chopped	2
1 tbsp	Dijon mustard	15 mL
2 tbsp	balsamic vinegar	30 mL
4	chicken legs	4
	freshly ground pepper	

1 Place 2 tbsp (30 mL) oil in mixing bowl. Add remaining ingredients, except chicken, and mix very well.

2 Place chicken in roasting pan and cover with marinade. Cover and refrigerate 1 hour. Turn chicken legs over 4 times.

3 Preheat oven to 350°F (180°C).

4 Remove chicken legs from marinade and pat dry. Heat remaining oil in sauté pan over medium heat. Add chicken and cook 8 minutes over low heat. Turn legs over often to prevent charring.

5 Transfer chicken to oven and finish cooking 35 to 40 minutes, or adjust time according to size. Baste chicken with marinade during cooking process.

6 Test if chicken is done by piercing flesh with metal skewer. Juices should run clear.

7 Serve with a fresh garden salad.

Marinated Chicken Breasts with Rosemary
(4 servings)

2	whole boneless chicken breasts	2
½ cup	dry white wine	125 mL
3 tbsp	olive oil	45 mL
1 tsp	basil	5 mL
1 tsp	rosemary	5 mL
2	garlic cloves, peeled	2
¼ cup	olive oil	50 mL
½ lb	fresh mushroom caps, cleaned	225 g
24	cherry tomatoes, halved	24
1 tbsp	chopped fresh parsley	15 mL
	salt and pepper	

1 Skin chicken and cut into pieces 1 in (2.5 cm) wide. Place in bowl with wine, 3 tbsp (45 mL) olive oil, basil, rosemary and garlic. Season well, mix and cover with plastic wrap. Marinate 1 hour in refrigerator.

2 Heat half of remaining measure of oil in frying pan over high heat. Add half of chicken and stir-fry 2 to 3 minutes over high heat. Remove chicken from pan and set aside.

3 Add remaining chicken to hot pan and repeat cooking process. Set aside with first batch of cooked chicken.

4 Add remaining oil to pan. When hot, cook mushroom caps 3 minutes over high heat. Add tomatoes, season and cook another 2 minutes.

5 Return chicken to pan and add parsley. Mix and cook 1 minute before serving. Accompany with rice, if desired.

Chicken Fast-Fry Fricassée
(4 servings)

2	whole boneless chicken breasts	2
3 tbsp	olive oil	45 mL
3	tomatoes, peeled, seeded and chopped	3
2	garlic cloves, peeled and sliced	2
2	anchovy fillets, rinsed, drained and chopped	2
1 tbsp	chopped fresh basil	15 mL
½ cup	dry white wine	125 mL
	salt and pepper	
	pinch of savory	

1 Skin chicken and cut in strips about ½ in (1 cm) wide. Heat half of oil in large frying pan over medium heat. Add half of chicken and season well. Cook 3 to 4 minutes over high heat, turning chicken over once. Remove chicken and set aside; keep warm.

2 Heat remaining oil in pan. When hot, add remaining chicken and repeat cooking process. Set aside with first batch of cooked chicken.

3 Add tomatoes, garlic, anchovies and seasonings to hot pan. Cook 4 minutes over high heat.

4 Add wine and season well. Continue cooking 2 minutes. Return chicken to pan; simmer 2 minutes over low heat and serve. Accompany with pasta, if desired.

Breast of Chicken Balsamic
(4 servings)

2	whole boneless chicken breasts	2
¼ cup	butter	50 mL
4	shallots, peeled and sliced	4
¾ cup	balsamic vinegar	175 mL
1 tbsp	honey	15 mL
	salt and pepper	

1 Skin chicken and split into halves. Season with salt and pepper.

2 Heat 2 tbsp (30 mL) butter in sauté pan over medium heat. Add chicken and cook 8 to 10 minutes or adjust time according to size. Turn breasts over halfway through cooking.

3 Remove chicken from pan and keep warm.

4 Add shallots to pan and sauté 2 minutes over medium heat. Pour in vinegar and honey. Cook until liquid becomes syrupy. Remove pan from heat and stir in remaining butter.

5 Pour over chicken and serve with a green salad.

Chicken and Seafood
(4 servings)

2	whole boneless chicken breasts	2
¼ cup	butter	50 mL
½ lb	fresh shrimp, peeled and deveined	225 g
1½ cups	croutons	375 mL
1 tbsp	chopped fresh parsley	15 mL
	juice of 1 lemon	
	salt and pepper	

1 Skin chicken, split into halves and remove fat.

2 Heat 3 tbsp (45 mL) butter in sauté pan over medium heat. Add chicken and lemon juice; season well. Cover and cook 10 minutes over low heat or adjust time according to size. Turn breasts over twice.

3 When cooked, remove chicken from pan and keep warm.

4 Add remaining butter to pan and increase heat to high. Add shrimp and cook 3 minutes. Season well.

5 Add croutons and parsley; cook 2 minutes.

6 Pour shrimp mixture over chicken breasts and serve with pasta, if desired.

Chicken Paprika
(4 servings)

3 ½ lb	cleaned chicken, cut in 6 pieces	1.6 kg
3 tbsp	olive oil	45 mL
1	large Spanish onion, peeled and thinly sliced	1
2 tbsp	paprika	30 mL
2 tbsp	flour	30 mL
1 ½ cups	chicken stock, heated	375 mL
2	tomatoes, peeled, seeded and chopped	2
2	garlic cloves, peeled, crushed and chopped	2
	salt and pepper	
	sour cream and chopped fresh chives	

1 Skin chicken pieces and season well. Heat oil in sauté pan over medium heat. Add chicken and brown on all sides for 8 minutes.

2 Add onion; cook 10 minutes over low heat.

3 Remove chicken breasts from pan and set aside; keep warm.

4 Add paprika to pan with remaining chicken and mix well. Cook 3 minutes. Add flour and mix again.

5 Pour in chicken stock and mix well. Season, add tomatoes and garlic, and continue cooking 8 minutes over low heat.

6 Return chicken breasts to pan; simmer 3 minutes. Serve with sour cream and chives. Accompany with rice and julienned vegetables, if desired.

Heat oil in sauté pan over medium heat. Add chicken and brown on all sides for 8 minutes.

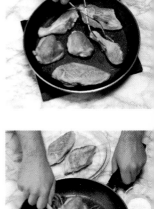

Add onion; cook 10 minutes over low heat. Remove chicken breasts from pan and set aside; keep warm.

Pour in chicken stock and mix well. Season, add tomatoes and garlic, and continue cooking 8 minutes over low heat.

Return chicken breasts to pan; simmer 3 minutes.

Chicken Legs Louis
(4 servings)

4	large chicken legs	4
2	large garlic cloves, peeled	2
1 cup	flour	250 mL
½ tsp	each: black and white pepper	2 mL
¼ tsp	cayenne pepper	1 mL
¼ tsp	ground ginger	1 mL
¼ cup	vegetable oil	50 mL
2 cups	chicken stock, heated	500 mL
2 tbsp	butter	30 mL
½ cup	each: diced onion, diced celery and diced bell pepper	125 mL

Preheat oven to 350°F (180°C).

1 Cut chicken legs in half at the joint, between the thigh and the drumstick. Remove skin. Rub meat with garlic cloves, then discard garlic. Place ¾ cup (175 mL) of flour in clean plastic bag. Add seasonings and shake to mix. Add chicken legs and shake to coat well.

2 Heat oil in cast iron sauté pan over medium heat. Add chicken and cook 6 minutes on each side. Remove chicken from pan and set aside. Strain oil through sieve lined with cheesecloth into bowl. Pour oil back into pan.

3 Return pan to stove over medium heat. Add remaining flour and brown, stirring constantly. Do not let roux burn. Reduce heat to low. Pour in chicken stock and simmer 2 minutes over low heat.

4 Heat butter in another frying pan over medium heat. Add vegetables and cook 5 minutes. Transfer to sauce in cast iron pan.

5 Place chicken in sauce, cover and cook 40 to 45 minutes in oven or adjust time according to size. Serve with rice and carrots, if desired.

Country Chicken with White Wine
(4 servings)

3½ lb	cleaned chicken, cut in 6 pieces	1.6 kg
2 tbsp	olive oil	30 mL
24	pearl onions, peeled	24
24	Parisienne potatoes, cooked 6 minutes	24
1	large red bell pepper, diced large	1
2	garlic cloves, peeled, crushed and chopped	2
1 cup	dry white wine	250 mL
1 tbsp	chopped fresh basil	15 mL
	salt and pepper	

1 Skin chicken pieces and season well. Heat oil in sauté pan over medium heat. Add chicken. Cook 10 minutes over low heat, turning pieces over once or twice.

2 Add pearl onions and continue cooking 8 minutes over low heat. Turn chicken pieces over once.

3 Remove chicken breasts from pan and set aside.

4 Add Parisienne potatoes, bell pepper and garlic; season well. Continue cooking 8 minutes.

5 Return chicken breasts to pan and continue cooking 2 minutes. Remove chicken and vegetables from pan and keep warm on serving platter.

6 Increase heat under sauté pan to high and pour in wine. Cook 3 minutes.

7 Pour sauce over chicken, sprinkle with fresh basil and serve. Accompany with green beans, if desired.

Chicken Legs with Hot Tomato Sauce
(4 servings)

4	large chicken legs	4
½ tsp	black pepper	2 mL
¼ tsp	cayenne pepper	1 mL
½ tsp	white pepper	2 mL
¼ tsp	chili powder	1 mL
¼ tsp	salt	1 mL
2 tbsp	vegetable oil	30 mL
1	onion, peeled and chopped	1
½	celery stalk, diced	½
1	red bell pepper, diced	1
1	jalapeño pepper, seeded and chopped	1
3	tomatoes, peeled, seeded and chopped	3
1 cup	tomato sauce	250 mL
	generous pinch of sugar	

Preheat oven to 350°F (180°C).

1 Cut chicken legs in half at the joint, between the thigh and the drumstick. Remove skin.

2 Mix all seasonings, except sugar, together in small bowl. Rub mixture into flesh of chicken.

3 Heat oil in cast iron sauté pan over medium heat. Add chicken and cook 6 minutes on each side over low heat. Remove chicken and set aside.

4 Add onion, celery, bell pepper and jalapeño pepper to hot pan. Cook 3 minutes. Add tomatoes, tomato sauce and sugar; season well. Cook 6 minutes over medium heat.

5 Place chicken in sauce, cover and cook 40 to 45 minutes in oven or adjust time according to size. Stir twice during cooking.

6 When cooked, remove chicken from pan and set aside. Place pan on stove over medium heat and cook 2 minutes.

7 Return chicken to sauce in pan and simmer 2 minutes before serving.

good added sliced mushrooms 11-07-04

Chicken with Lemon Sauce
(4 servings)

2	whole boneless chicken breasts	2
2 tbsp	butter	30 mL
1 tbsp	olive oil	15 mL
1	garlic clove, peeled and sliced	1
1 1/2 cups	chicken stock, heated	375 mL
1 tbsp	cornstarch	15 mL
2 tbsp	cold water	30 mL
1 tsp	soy sauce	5 mL
1 tsp	grated lemon zest	5 mL
	juice of 1 1/2 lemons	
	salt and pepper	

1 Skin chicken and cut in strips about 1/2 in (1 cm) wide. Heat half of butter and half of oil in wok or large frying pan over high heat. Add half of chicken and season well. Stir-fry 3 to 4 minutes over high heat. Remove chicken and set aside.

2 Heat remaining butter and oil in wok. Add remaining chicken to hot pan and repeat cooking process. Set aside with first batch of cooked chicken.

3 Add garlic to wok and stir-fry 20 seconds. Pour in lemon juice and chicken stock; cook 2 to 3 minutes over high heat.

4 Dilute cornstarch in cold water; stir into sauce. Add soy sauce, season and mix well.

5 Return chicken to sauce in pan and stir in lemon zest. Simmer 1 minute and serve with steamed rice.

Fried Chicken Strips with Vegetables
(4 servings)

2	whole small boneless chicken breasts	2
2 tbsp	soy sauce	30 mL
¼ cup	dry white wine	50 mL
2	garlic cloves, peeled, crushed and chopped	2
¼ cup	vegetable oil	50 mL
½ lb	fresh mushrooms, cleaned and thickly sliced	225 g
½	zucchini, cut in sticks	½
1	small bunch asparagus, cooked al dente and cut in 1-in (2.5-cm) lengths	1
2	carrots, cut in sticks and cooked al dente	2
½ cup	pine nuts	125 mL
1 cup	chicken stock, heated	250 mL
½ tsp	cornstarch	2 mL
1 tbsp	cold water	15 mL
	pinch crushed chilies	
	salt and pepper	

1 Skin chicken and cut in strips about ¼ in (5 mm) wide. Place in bowl with soy sauce, wine, garlic, crushed chilies and pepper. Marinate 15 minutes.

2 Heat half of oil in wok or large frying pan over high heat. When hot, add chicken strips and stir-fry 2 to 3 minutes over high heat. Remove chicken and set aside.

3 Add remaining oil to pan. When hot, add mushrooms and zucchini. Stir-fry 3 minutes over high heat. Season well.

4 Add remaining vegetables and pine nuts; cook 1 minute.

5 Pour in chicken stock. Dilute cornstarch in cold water; stir into sauce. Return chicken strips to wok, mix well and cook another 30 seconds to reheat. Serve with noodles, if desired.

Brandy-Spiked Chicken Fry
(4 servings)

2	**whole small boneless chicken breasts**	2
3 tbsp	**olive oil**	45 mL
1	**yellow bell pepper, cut in strips**	1
1	**red bell pepper, cut in strips**	1
1	**bunch asparagus, cooked al dente and cut in 1-in (2.5-cm) lengths**	1
¼ lb	**green beans, cooked and cut in half**	125 g
1 cup	**chicken stock, heated**	250 mL
2 tbsp	**teriyaki sauce**	30 mL
2 tbsp	**brandy**	30 mL
1 tsp	**cornstarch**	5 mL
1 tbsp	**cold water**	15 mL
	salt and pepper	

1 Skin chicken and cut in strips about ¼ in (5 mm) wide.

2 Heat half of oil in large frying pan over high heat. Add chicken and season well. Cook 2 to 3 minutes over high heat, turning chicken over once. Remove chicken and set aside.

3 Add remaining oil to pan. When hot, add all vegetables. Season and stir-fry 1 to 2 minutes. Remove vegetables and set aside.

4 Mix chicken stock with teriyaki and brandy. Pour into frying pan. Dilute cornstarch in cold water; add to sauce. Mix well and cook 20 seconds.

5 Return chicken and vegetables to pan; cook another 20 seconds and serve. Accompany with rice, if desired.

Ginger-Spiced Chicken Stir-Fry
(4 servings)

2	whole small boneless chicken breasts	2
2 tbsp	chopped fresh ginger	30 mL
2	shallots, peeled and chopped	2
3 tbsp	teriyaki sauce	45 mL
¼ cup	sherry wine	50 mL
3 tbsp	vegetable oil	45 mL
1	red bell pepper, thinly sliced	1
1	small zucchini, sliced	1
2	garlic cloves, peeled and sliced	2
1	chili pepper, seeded and chopped	1
6	cherry tomatoes, halved	6
1 ½ cups	chicken stock, heated	375 mL
½ tsp	cornstarch	2 mL
1 tbsp	cold water	15 mL
	salt and pepper	

1 Skin chicken and slice into strips ¼ in (5 mm) wide; place in bowl. Add ginger, shallots, teriyaki and sherry; season with salt and pepper. Cover with plastic wrap and marinate in refrigerator for 30 minutes.

2 Heat half of oil in wok or deep sauté pan over high heat. When hot, add chicken strips and stir-fry 2 to 3 minutes over high heat. Remove chicken and set aside.

3 Add remaining oil to wok. When hot, add vegetables. Stir-fry 2 to 3 minutes over high heat.

4 Pour in chicken stock. Dilute cornstarch in cold water; mix into sauce. Cook 30 seconds. Return chicken to wok to reheat, then serve immediately with rice.

Chicken with Snow Peas and Broccoli
(4 servings)

2	**whole boneless chicken breasts**	2
3 tbsp	**vegetable oil**	45 mL
1	**head broccoli, in florets and blanched**	1
½ lb	**snow peas, blanched**	225 g
12	**cooked pearl onions**	12
2	**garlic cloves, peeled, crushed and chopped**	2
1 tbsp	**chopped fresh ginger**	15 mL
1½ cups	**chicken stock, heated**	375 mL
1 tsp	**soy sauce**	5 mL
1 tsp	**sugar**	5 mL
1 tbsp	**vinegar**	15 mL
1 tsp	**cornstarch**	5 mL
1 tbsp	**cold water**	15 mL
	salt and pepper	

1 Skin chicken and cut in strips about ½ in (1 cm) wide. Heat half of oil in large frying pan over high heat. Add chicken and season well. Cook 3 to 4 minutes over high heat, turning chicken over once.

2 Remove chicken from pan and set aside; keep warm.

3 Add remaining oil to pan. When hot, add vegetables and cook 1 minute over high heat. Remove from pan and set aside.

4 Add garlic and ginger to hot pan; sauté 30 seconds. Pour in chicken stock and add soy sauce, sugar and vinegar; mix well. Cook 4 minutes over medium heat.

5 Dilute cornstarch in cold water; stir into sauce. Reduce heat to low. Return chicken and vegetables to pan; correct seasoning. Simmer 2 minutes and serve with rice.

Breast of Chicken with Green Peppercorns
(4 servings)

2	whole boneless chicken breasts	2
¼ cup	butter	50 mL
1	shallot, peeled and chopped	1
½ lb	fresh mushroom caps, cleaned and quartered	225 g
½ cup	dry white wine	125 mL
2 cups	chicken stock, heated	500 mL
3 tbsp	green peppercorns	45 mL
1 tbsp	cornstarch	15 mL
3 tbsp	cold water	45 mL
	salt and cayenne pepper	

1 Skin chicken and split into halves. Heat half of butter in sauté pan over medium heat. Add chicken, season and partly cover. Cook 8 to 10 minutes over low heat, turning breasts over once.

2 Remove chicken from pan and set aside.

3 Add remaining butter to hot pan. Add shallot and mushrooms; season well. Cook 4 minutes over high heat.

4 Pour in wine and cook 2 minutes. Add chicken stock and mashed peppercorns; continue cooking 4 minutes over medium heat.

5 Dilute cornstarch in cold water. Stir into sauce. Return chicken to pan and simmer 3 minutes over low heat.

6 Serve with glazed baby carrots, asparagus and rice, if desired.

Tasty Chicken Burgers
(4 servings)

1 ¼ lb	ground chicken	600 g
3	garlic cloves, blanched	3
3 tbsp	chutney	45 mL
2 tbsp	vegetable oil	30 mL
	few drops hot pepper sauce	
	salt and freshly ground pepper	

1 Place all ingredients, except oil, in food processor. Blend just to incorporate, then shape into small patties.

2 Heat oil in large frying pan over medium heat. When hot, add patties and cook 7 to 8 minutes over medium heat or adjust time according to thickness. Turn patties over halfway through cooking.

3 Serve on toasted buns with fresh tomato slices, lettuce and chutney.

Marinated Fried Chicken Strips
(4 servings)

2	**whole boneless chicken breasts**	2
3 tbsp	**olive oil**	45 mL
3 tbsp	**lime juice**	45 mL
2	**garlic cloves, peeled, crushed and chopped**	2
1/2 tsp	**oregano**	2 mL
1/4 tsp	**thyme**	I mL
1/2 tsp	**marjoram**	2 mL
1 1/2 cups	**seasoned flour**	375 mL
2	**large eggs, beaten**	2
2 cups	**breadcrumbs**	500 mL
	salt and pepper	
	peanut oil for deep frying	

1 Skin chicken and cut meat into thick strips. Set aside in deep plate.

2 Mix oil, lime juice, garlic and seasonings together. Pour over chicken, mix and marinate I hour in refrigerator.

3 Place seasoned flour in clean plastic bag. Add chicken strips and shake until coated.

4 Dip chicken in beaten eggs, then coat in breadcrumbs.

5 Deep fry in hot peanut oil until golden brown and cooked through; about 3 to 4 minutes, depending on size. Drain on paper towel before serving.

Breaded Chicken Strips
(4 servings)

1 ½	whole boneless chicken breasts	1 ½
1 cup	flour	250 mL
2	large eggs, beaten	2
1 ½ cups	breadcrumbs	375 mL
½ cup	vegetable oil	125 mL
1 cup	sour cream	250 mL
2 tbsp	chopped fresh chives	30 mL
	salt and pepper	
	cayenne pepper to taste	
	pinch of paprika	

Preheat oven to 375°F (190°C).

1 Skin chicken and trim off all fat. Cut in strips about ½ in (1 cm) wide.

2 Place chicken in bowl. Add all seasonings, except chives, and mix well. Dredge chicken in flour then dip in beaten eggs. Coat thoroughly in breadcrumbs.

3 Heat oil in cast iron pan over high heat. When hot, cook chicken in 2 or 3 batches until golden brown; about 3 to 4 minutes.

4 Remove cooked batches with slotted spoon and keep hot in oven. Mix sour cream with chives and serve with chicken.

Stuffed Guinea Hens
(4 servings)

2	guinea hens	2
⅓ cup	butter	75 mL
1	onion, peeled and chopped	1
2	garlic cloves, peeled, crushed and chopped	2
1	thin slice smoked Virginia ham, finely chopped	1
1 tbsp	chopped fresh parsley	15 mL
1 tbsp	chopped fresh tarragon	15 mL
1 cup	breadcrumbs	250 mL
1	small egg, beaten	1
	salt and pepper	
	pinch of thyme	

Preheat oven to 450°F (230°C).

1 Clean hens and dry thoroughly. Season inside and out; set aside.

2 Heat 2 tbsp (30 mL) butter in small frying pan over medium heat. Add onion and garlic; cook 3 minutes over low heat. Add ham, parsley, tarragon and thyme; cook 30 seconds. Transfer mixture to bowl.

3 Add breadcrumbs and mix well. Add beaten egg, season and mix again.

4 Stuff hens with mixture. Truss for roasting. Spread remaining butter over skin and arrange hens in roasting pan. Cook 30 to 40 minutes in oven or adjust time according to size. Baste every 12 minutes.

5 Serve with vegetables.

Heat 2 tbsp (30 mL) butter in small frying pan over medium heat. Add onion and garlic; cook 3 minutes over low heat. Add ham, parsley, tarragon and thyme; cook 30 seconds.

Add breadcrumbs and mix well. Add beaten egg, season and mix again.

Stuff hens with mixture.

Truss hens for roasting.

Roast Guinea Hens with Bacon
(4 servings)

2	**guinea hens**	2
2 tbsp	**butter**	30 mL
1 tbsp	**olive oil**	15 mL
1 tbsp	**chopped fresh oregano**	15 mL
½ tsp	**coriander**	2 mL
½ tsp	**sage**	2 mL
12	**slices bacon**	12
4	**shallots, peeled and chopped**	4
1½ cups	**dry white wine**	375 mL
	salt and pepper	

Preheat oven to 425°F (220°C).

1 Clean hens and dry thoroughly. Season inside and out. Divide butter between cavities; truss for roasting.

2 Rub olive oil over skin. Mix seasonings together and sprinkle over hens. Drape bacon slices over birds.

3 Arrange in roasting pan and cook 20 minutes. As soon as bacon is well cooked, remove slices and discard. Continue cooking hens 10 to 20 minutes or adjust time according to size.

4 When cooked, remove hens from pan and keep warm.

5 Place roasting pan on stove. Discard three quarters of fat remaining in pan. Add shallots to pan and cook 1 minute over medium heat.

6 Pour in white wine and increase heat to high; cook 3 minutes. Correct seasoning. Slice hens and serve with sauce. Accompany with vegetables and rice, if desired.

Rock Cornish Hens with Rice Stuffing
(4 servings)

4	Rock Cornish hens	4
¼ cup	butter	50 mL
1	onion, peeled and finely chopped	1
1	garlic clove, peeled, crushed and chopped	1
1 tbsp	chopped fresh tarragon	15 mL
1 cup	long grain rice, rinsed	250 mL
2 cups	chicken stock, heated	500 mL
½ cup	chopped walnuts	125 mL
	salt and pepper	

Preheat oven to 450°F (230°C).

1 Clean hens and dry thoroughly. Season inside and out; set aside.

2 Heat 1 tbsp (15 mL) butter in saucepan over medium heat. Add onion, garlic and tarragon; cook 3 minutes over low heat.

3 Mix in rice and cook 2 minutes. Pour in chicken stock, mix and season with pepper. Cover and cook 18 to 20 minutes over low heat. Rice is cooked when liquid is absorbed.

4 Stir walnuts and 1 tsp (5 mL) of butter into cooked rice.

5 Stuff hens with mixture and truss for roasting. Spread remaining butter over skin and arrange hens in roasting pan. Cook 30 to 40 minutes in oven or adjust time according to size. Baste every 10 minutes.

6 Serve with caramelized apple slices. Accompany with spinach and carrots, if desired.

Roast Guinea Hens
(4 servings)

2	**guinea hens**	2
¼ cup	**butter, softened**	50 mL
2	**shallots, peeled and chopped**	2
24	**seedless green grapes**	24
1½ cups	**chicken stock, heated**	375 mL
1 tbsp	**chopped fresh basil**	15 mL
1 tbsp	**chopped fresh tarragon**	15 mL
1 tbsp	**cornstarch**	15 mL
3 tbsp	**cold water**	45 mL
	salt and pepper	

Preheat oven to 450°F (230°C).

1 Clean hens and dry thoroughly. Season inside and out; truss for roasting.

2 Spread butter over skin and arrange hens in roasting pan. Cook 30 to 40 minutes in oven or adjust time according to size. Baste every 12 minutes and turn hens over during cooking.

3 When cooked, remove hens from pan and set aside; keep warm.

4 Place roasting pan on stove over medium heat. Add shallots and grapes; cook 2 minutes.

5 Add chicken stock and herbs; cook 2 minutes.

6 Dilute cornstarch in cold water; stir into sauce. Simmer 2 minutes over low heat. Serve with hens. Accompany with green beans, chopped apple and turnip, if desired.

Quails with Spicy Rice Stuffing
(2 to 4 servings)

SPICY RICE STUFFING:

3 tbsp	butter	45 mL
1	onion, peeled and chopped	1
1	garlic clove, peeled and sliced	1
¼ tsp	black pepper	1 mL
¼ tsp	cayenne pepper	1 mL
¼ tsp	white pepper	1 mL
1	chili pepper, seeded and chopped	1
1 cup	long grain rice, rinsed	250 mL
1½ cups	chicken stock, heated	375 mL
	salt	

Preheat oven to 350°F (180°C).

1 Heat butter in ovenproof casserole over medium heat. Add onion, garlic, spices and chili pepper. Mix and cook 2 minutes.

2 Add rice and season with salt. Cook 3 minutes to evaporate liquid. When rice starts to stick to bottom of pan, pour in chicken stock. Bring to boil, then cover and cook 18 minutes in oven.

QUAILS:

4	quails, cleaned	4
3 tbsp	melted butter	45 mL
	salt and pepper	

Preheat oven to 425°F (220°C).

1 Season quails inside and out. Fill cavities with Spicy Rice Stuffing. Truss for roasting.

2 Brush skin with butter and place quails in roasting pan. Cook 25 to 30 minutes or adjust time according to size, basting occasionally.

3 Serve with fresh vegetables.

Grilled Quails
(2 to 4 servings)

4	quails, cleaned	4
2	garlic cloves, peeled and halved	2
¼ cup	teriyaki sauce	50 mL
¼ cup	sake wine	50 mL
2 tbsp	honey	30 mL
¼ tsp	ground ginger	1 mL
¼ tsp	chili powder	1 mL
3 tbsp	olive oil	45 mL
	salt and pepper	

1 Using poultry shears, cut through backbone of quails to split in half. Rub flesh with garlic and season well. Place in shallow dish.

2 Mix remaining ingredients together and pour over quails. Marinate in refrigerator for 2 hours, turning meat over several times.

Preheat oven to 400°F (200°C).

3 Change oven setting to broil. Arrange quails, skin-side-up, in roasting pan. Broil 12 minutes, basting frequently.

4 Turn quails over and continue cooking 10 minutes or adjust time according to size. Baste frequently.

5 Serve with a spicy rice.

Garlic Butter to Serve with Chicken

(yield: 1/2 lb (225 g))

¹/₂ lb	butter, softened	225 g
1	shallot, peeled and finely chopped	1
2	large garlic cloves, peeled, crushed and chopped	2
1 tsp	chopped fresh parsley	5 mL
	few drops Tabasco sauce	
	salt and freshly ground pepper	
	lemon juice to taste	

1 Place all ingredients in large bowl. Using wooden spoon, mix together until well incorporated.

2 Mound butter on large sheet of doubled aluminum foil. Form butter into cylindrical shape and roll up in foil. Twist ends shut.

3 Chill in refrigerator until firm or freeze for later use.

4 To use, simply unroll foil and slice off desired amount of garlic butter. Wrap tightly again and store in freezer.

Zesty Marinade for Chicken

¹/₄ cup	lime juice	50 mL
¹/₂ cup	olive oil	125 mL
3	garlic cloves, peeled and sliced	3
1	jalapeño pepper, seeded and chopped	1
3 tbsp	ground pepper	45 mL
5	fresh sorrel leaves	5
¹/₂ tsp	thyme	2 mL

1 Place all ingredients in saucepan. Mix well and cook 3 minutes over medium heat.

2 Pour over chicken and marinate at least 1 hour in refrigerator.

Use this marinade for grilling or sauté methods of cooking.

Teriyaki-Madeira Marinade

¼ cup	teriyaki sauce	50 mL
1 tbsp	honey	15 mL
1 tbsp	soy sauce	15 mL
2	garlic cloves, peeled and sliced	2
¼ cup	Madeira wine	50 mL
	freshly ground pepper	

1 Mix all ingredients together in bowl.

2 Pour over chicken and marinate 1 hour in refrigerator.

Use this marinade for grilling or sauté methods of cooking. It can also be used to baste a whole chicken during roasting.

Seasoned Rub

1 tsp	olive oil	5 mL
1 tbsp	cumin seeds	15 mL
1 tsp	coriander seeds	5 mL
5	blanched garlic cloves, peeled and puréed	5
1	jalapeño pepper, seeded and finely chopped	1
1 tsp	thyme	5 mL
1 tsp	celery seeds	5 mL
½ tsp	chili powder	2 mL
3 tbsp	lime juice	45 mL

1 Heat oil in small frying pan over medium heat. When hot, add cumin and coriander seeds; cook 1 minute or until golden brown.

2 Add remaining ingredients, except lime juice, to pan. Mix well and cook 1 minute.

3 Rub mixture into scored flesh of chicken. Drizzle lime juice over and prepare to cook chicken.

Use this mixture for roasting a whole chicken or chicken pieces.

Traditional Wine Marinade

¼ cup	olive oil	50 mL
½ cup	dry white wine	125 mL
1	garlic clove, peeled and sliced	1
1 tbsp	Dijon mustard	15 mL
1 tbsp	wine vinegar	15 mL
½ tsp	thyme	2 mL
1 tsp	tarragon	5 mL
1 tsp	basil	5 mL
	freshly ground pepper	

1 Place all ingredients in bowl and mix together well.

2 Pour over chicken and marinate in refrigerator.

Use this marinade for any cooking method.

Sauce for Roast Chicken
(4 to 6 servings)

1	onion, peeled and chopped	1
½	celery stalk, diced small	½
1	carrot, pared and diced small	1
3 tbsp	flour	45 mL
2 cups	chicken stock, heated	500 mL
½ tsp	thyme	2 mL
¼ tsp	marjoram	1 mL
½ tsp	celery seeds	2 mL
	freshly ground pepper	

1 Make sauce as soon as roast chicken is done. Discard half of fat remaining in roasting pan.

2 Place roasting pan with remaining fat on stove over medium heat. Add onion, celery and carrot; cook 5 minutes. Stir frequently.

3 Sprinkle in flour and mix well. Cook 2 minutes over low heat.

4 Pour in chicken stock and incorporate with whisk. Add seasonings and cook sauce 6 to 8 minutes over low heat.

5 Strain sauce and serve in gravy boat with roast chicken.

Index